Irish Eyes Are Still Smiling
Trivia, legends, and lore of St. Patrick's Day

An Outhouse Trivia Book

By Christopher Forest

♣ ♣ ♣

Dear readers,

Thanks so much for reading this second edition of Outhouse Book *Irish Eyes Are Smiling*. In this book, you will learn about the history of one of the most popular holidays – St. Patrick's Day. From facts about St. Patrick, to trivia about Ireland, and little know folklore, this book will have you speaking Blarney in a matter of hours.

Hopefully you enjoy this brand of specialized reader. It is designed for those of you who like to have a sense of accomplishment, but have limited time to read. These quick readers can be completed in one session....even in the privacy of your own "outhouse."

We hope you enjoy! Happy reading!!!

Sincerely,
The Outhouse Staff

♣ ♣ ♣

Outhouse Books

Summary: A collection of interesting facts, trivia, and tidbits about St. Patrick's Day.

Author: Christopher Forest
Editor: Melissa Forest

ISBN: 978-1530293711

Outhouse Books
Danvers, MA 01923
1 2 3 4 5 6 7 8 9 0 1

♣ ♣ ♣

St. Patrick's Day at a Glance

May joy and peace surround you, contentment latch your door, and happiness be
with you now and bless you evermore.
-Traditional Irish Blessing

♣ ♣ ♣

So why is St. Patrick's Day celebrated March 17th. It is believed that St. Patrick actually died on that day in 461 AD.

♣ ♣ ♣

It also happened on March 17th

- 45 BC: Julius Caesar wins his last war victory, defeating Titus Labienus and Pompey the Younger

- 1805: Napoleon declares himself king of Italy

- 1902: Legendary golfer Bobby Jones is born

- 1919: Nat King Cole is born

- 1941: The National Gallery of Art is open

- 1948: The United Kingdom, France, and Belelux sign the Treaty of Brussels, the forerunner to NATO

- 1963: Mount Agung erupts on Bali

♣ ♣ ♣

"Slainte" is a popular Irish term. It is actually the Irish blessing for health. It is pronounced "SLAN-cha." The proper response is "do dheagh slainte," which means "your good health."

There are several other versions of the saying.

"Air do shlainte" means "on your health."

"Slainte mhor" means "great health."

♣ ♣ ♣

What to celebrate St. Patrick's Day American style? Well, you can go to...

• Shamrock, Texas
• Shamrock, Oklahoma
• Shamrock Lakes, Indiana
• Irishtown, Illinois
• Emerald Isle, North Carolina

There is one town named St. Patrick's in the United States. It is in the "Show Me State" of Missouri.

♣ ♣ ♣

Want to travel to Dublin in the United States?

Well, you will find one in the following thirteen states: California, Georgia, Indiana, Kentucky, Maryland, Michigan, Mississippi, New Hampshire, North Carolina, Ohio, Pennsylvania, Texas, and Virginia. The locations in Kentucky, Maryland, and Michigan may be hard to find because they are unincorporated or are incorporated into other towns.

♣ ♣ ♣

More of It Happened On St. Patrick's Day

471 : St. Patrick passes to his heavenly reward

1521: Ferdinand Magellan discovers the Philippines

1776: British evacuate Boston

1836: Slavery is abolished in Texas

1854: A U.S. city (Worcester, MA) purchases park land for the first time

1905: Franklin Delano Roosevelt and Eleanor Roosevelt marry

1917: Czar Nicolas II is forced to abdicate the throne of Russia

1963: Bob Cousy plays his last game for the – you guessed it – Boston Celtics

1969: Golda Meir becomes the prime minister of Israel

1973: The new London Bridge is open

♣ ♣ ♣

St. Patrick's Symbols

"May your blessings outnumber the shamrocks that grow,
And may trouble avoid you wherever you go."

-Traditional Irish prayer

Wearing the green! The color green became associated with St. Patrick's Day in the 1800s. According to Irish folklore, fairies and other legendary creatures wear the color green.

♣ ♣ ♣

The color green now stands for the symbol of hope in Ireland. But, long ago it was a color to be feared. Because the fairy folk often wore green, it was believed if a person wore too much of it, the fairies might kidnap that person.

♣ ♣ ♣

What is a shamrock? The word "shamrock" comes from the Gaelic word "seamróg", which means "young clover."

There are four species of clover that are often associated with the shamrock. They are...

1. The black medic
2. The white clover
3. The hope clover
4. The wood sorrel

♣ ♣ ♣

The mother lode! Shamrocks, or clovers, are a common staple for the holiday. While people often look for four-leaf clovers, keep your eyes open for shamrocks even larger. According to the Guinness Book, the largest amount of leaves found on one clover is a whopping 14! Talk about lucky!

♣ ♣ ♣

Shamrocks were used by St. Patrick to help teach about the Holy Trinity of God, Jesus, and the Holy Spirit. Likely, he knew that the Druids of the region used the shamrock to teach about the three forms of the goddess, Ana as maid, mother, and crone. Patrick probably adapted its use for his religion.

♣ ♣ ♣

Playing Irish music on St. Patrick's Day is an ancient custom that has stood the test of time. It dates back to days when music was used to tell the folklore of the Irish. When England gained control of the country, the government eventually banned the music under penalty of death because it often brought the residents of Ireland together and filled them with deep emotion.

Musical instruments popular in Irish music are flutes, whistles, trumpets, and Uilleann pipes.

♣ ♣ ♣

Uillean Pipes

While bagpipes are often associated with Scotland, the Irish have their version of bagpipes, too. The Irish pipes were used for centuries in Ireland (and scholars say at least 300 years before the most celebrated Irish instrument – the Irish harp - surfaced in the country). The pipes were originally called war pipes and were used to provide marching music for armies.

Overtime, the war pipes were replaced by the smaller Uillean pipes. They play two octaves instead of one octave played by war pipes. The air comes in by use of a bellows and exits through the different pipes.

♣ ♣ ♣

Harps have it! The harp is often associated with St. Patrick's Day because it is the symbol of Ireland.

The traditional Celtic harp is a triangular-shaped harp. These harps have existed since the 10th century. Some may have been made of iron, brass, gold, or silver.

One of the most celebrated Celtic harpists of all time is Turlough O'Carolan. He compiled a list of 220 compositions for the harp in the 1600s.

♣ ♣ ♣

Harps as a symbol

The Celtic Harp is an official symbol of Ireland. It is found on Irish money, the presidential flag, official uniforms, and some official beers.

The importance of the Celtic harp dates back to ancient Celtic mythology. According to legend, the first harp belonged to Dagda, a Celtic chief. His harp was stolen by the gods of darkness and cold. The gods of light and music helped him recover the harp and ever since, music has enlightened the land.

The Celtic harp, sometimes called Gaelic harp, has been found on carvings that date back to the twelfth century. The symbol became an official part of Ireland in the 1500s, when King Henry VIII (yes, that king known for so many other things) put it on Irish coins.

Today, the harp remains a symbol of the land. Often, the harp that is depicted in pictures, stamps, stickers, and artwork is known as the Brian Boru harp. This harp, which is on display in Trinity College in Dublin, is named for the king who owned it and is considered the oldest stringed instrument still in existence.

♣ ♣ ♣

The shillelagh is an Irish symbol attributed to the Gaelic god Dagda. The term actually means "staff of life," and it appeared to have special properties to help raise the dead.

Shillelaghs are traditionally made from the wood of an oak or blackthorn. They are designed to be black and shiny. A knob on the end is used for holding the shillelagh as a walking stick. However, it serves a double purpose for it can be used to strike people as a weapon if necessary.

According to some lore, shillelaghs were used to settle disputes in a gentleman's fashion.

♣ ♣ ♣

What's in a name? Leprechauns are popular sprits associated with St. Patrick's Day. The name is thought to have come from the word "leipreachan" which is a Gaelic word for a "mischievous sprite." Others trace the term to the word "leath brogan" which means a shoemaker. Still others believe it stems from "lobaircin" which means "small-bodied fellow."

♣ ♣ ♣

Leprechauns may seem bright and cheery, such as the one on *Lucky Charms* cereal boxes. Yet, this is purely an American invention. The traditional Irish version of the leprechaun paints a picture of a grumpy man (there were originally no women folk, which may explain why they were grumpy), who could perform evil as well as good.

♣ ♣ ♣

If you want to find a leprechaun, rumor has it to listen for the sound of shoe-making hammers while walking outside. Or look for rainbows in the middle of the woods. These are tell-tale signs that the wee folk are fast at work.

♣ ♣ ♣

Leprechauns could supposedly exchange their treasure for their freedom. But a person who catches a leprechaun must watch out. Take your eye off a fellow for a minute and he will disappear.

Some lore says you only have to steal a leprechaun's ring or amulet to buy his services.

A few stories even suggest that the leprechaun has the powers of a genie and can grant three wishes.

♣ ♣ ♣

Full of Blarney

The Blarney Stone, by virtue of being an Irish landmark, is often associated with St. Patrick's Day. Anyone who kisses it is believed to receive the gift of gab.

The Blarney Stone is actually a large piece of bluestone that was built into the battlements of Ireland's Blarney Castle; found about five miles northwest of Cork, Ireland.

The stone is believed to be a gift given by Robert the Bruce to Cormac McCarthy in 1314 in thanks for McCarthy's assistance during the Battle of Bannockburn. McCarthy was the King of Munster at the time and installed the stone in his castle.

No one knows when kissing the stone originated. However, some legends say an older woman cast a spell on the stone when a king of Munster rescued her from drowning. The spell ensured that anyone who kissed the stone at the castle's top would acquire speech that would gain the trust of other people.

♣ ♣ ♣

Shamrock Facts

• According to lore, a four-leaf clover has special meaning. One leaf stands for faith, another stands for hope, another stands for luck, and a fourth stands for love.

• Don't try it at home! One local shamrock superstition suggests that a young maiden should search for a four-leaf clover on St. Patty's day. If she finds one and eats it, legend says, she won't be unmarried for long.

• The most common "Irish shamrock" is actually called the white clover.

♣ ♣ ♣

Erin Go Braugh is a famous statement associated with St. Patrick's Day. It means "Ireland is Forever." It is the English translation of three words.

Erin comes from the Irish word Eire, which represents Ireland.

Go comes from the Irish word that translates roughly to the word "to," "until," or "up."

Bragh comes from the Irish word Brach, which means "until the end of time."

♣♣♣

Only on St. Patrick's Day

May the road rise up to meet you.
May the wind always be at your back.
May the sun shine warm upon your face,
And rains fall soft upon your fields.
And until we meet again,
May God hold you in the palm of His hand.

-Traditional Irish Blessing

♣ ♣ ♣

Staying mum? Many people add a touch of class on St. Patrick's Day by requesting white chrysanthemums dyed green and made into boutonnieres on the Irish holiday.

♣ ♣ ♣

Irish soda bread is a common staple on St. Patrick's Day. The main ingredients of the bread are flour, baking soda (or sodium bicarbonate), buttermilk, and salt. It gets its named because baking soda — and not yeast — is used to make the bread rise.

There are variations on the recipe throughout Ireland. For example, in Ulster, a version of soda bread is made with wheat flour and is sweetened. However, it is not called soda bread. In Ulster, that term is reserved for a white flour bread. In southern Ireland, soda bread is made with wheat flour and often called brown bread or brown soda bread.

♣ ♣ ♣

Want to have "Irish" desserts on St. Patrick's Day? Try these green concoctions:

1. Key lime pie
2. Lime Jello
3. Mint chocolate chip ice cream
4. Lemon meringue pie...with green food coloring

Would you refer traditional Irish desserts? Then try Gur. This is a pastry found in Dublin. Or, check out some Goody. This is a dessert made by boiling bread in milk and adding spices and sugar.

♣♣♣

Nothing like some corned beef and cabbage. CB and C is the traditional food of St. Patrick's Day! The corned beef comes from the top part and brisket of the cow. Because these cuts are so tough, a person cooking them will need to spend extra time preparing meals with corned beef.

♣ ♣ ♣

Where's the beef? Although corned beef is thought to be traditional, old-time Irish classic, it became associated with the holiday during the early 1900s. As a way to save money, New York immigrants substituted the standard Irish bacon with corned beef when serving it with cabbage.

Want a traditional Irish breakfast. Try some bangers and mash. This breakfast is most likely derived from multiple places in Great Britain. The bangers refer to sausage and the mash refers to baked potatoes...though home fries are often served now.

♣ ♣ ♣

White headed cabbage

Colannon is a food that some St. Patrick revelers eat on St. Patrick's Day. Traditionally associated with Halloween, it is often cabbage (or kale) mixed with mashed potatoes. The word is translated as "white-headed cabbage" in Gaelic.

In the ancient days, people would hide simple objects in colcannon to help predict the future ahead. After all, it was traditionally served on Halloween, which was once celebrated as the last day of the year. A person who discovered a ring would marry within the year. A person who located a thimble or button would not marry during the upcoming year. A person who found a coin would have a prosperous year ahead.

Some women even put colcannon in a sock and placed them on the handle of the door to their house for a special reason. The first eligible man that entered – according to legend – would become their spouse.

♣ ♣ ♣

Drowning the Shamrock was an old custom of letting a shamrock float on a glass (or shot glass) of whiskey and then taking a sip of it (of course, people should not eat the shamrock). The custom was used as a way to ensure a prosperous New Year.

The term now has a more colloquial meaning. It refers to people who go out to drink alcohol on St. Patrick's Day.

According to some, the tradition of drinking on St. Patrick's Day occurred as a way to honor an event in St. Patrick's life. Legends suggest that St. Patrick was visiting a pub owner who was known for underserving his whiskey. St. Patrick told the man that he needed to change his ways and serve his full measures of alcohol, or he might have to pay for his dishonesty. The next time Patrick visited the pub keeper, the glasses were overflowing.

♣ ♣ ♣

"Oh Danny Boy"

"Oh Danny Boy is a St. Patrick's Day staple. Here are a few things you may not have known about the legendary song.

• It is considered a British song, not Irish. The author of the lyrics was Frederick Edward Weatherly. He was a lawyer.

• He originally wrote the song in 1910, but had been unsuccessful with it. When he heard the music to "Londonderry Air" in 1912, he knew his words would go well with it. And a classic was born.

• Weatherly never visited Ireland.

• Many people wonder who Danny was. Well – though it may not have been him – Weatherly did have a son named Danny. Sadly, Danny passed away after the song was written while serving as a pilot in the RAF in World War I.

• The song was originally written to be performed by a female. A lyricist's note, located at the bottom of the sheet music, explained that male singers could substitute Danny Boy with "Eily Dear."

♣ ♣ ♣

Celebrating St. Patrick's Day

Bless those minding cattle,
And those minding sheep,
And those fishing the sea
While the rest of us sleep.

- Traditional Irish blessing

♣ ♣ ♣

The First Unofficial Parade

Boston may be the home to the St. Patrick's Day parade! The first official celebration of St. Patrick's Day is believed to have occurred in Boston. There, in 1737, people commemorated the Irish saint.

According to the stories of the day, the celebration was actually unplanned. A group known as the Irish Charitable Society had formed in the city. They had hoped to cultivate the spirit of unity among the Irish citizens of the colony and help to represent their needs.

On March 17th of that day, the group met in Boston and decided to celebrate the patron saint by holding a moving party, or parade, through the city. They encouraged everyone who wanted to join them in the festivities.

♣ ♣ ♣

The First Official Parade

The first Saint Patrick's Day parade was held on March 17, 1762. On that day, Irish soldiers enlisted in the British army and stationed in New York during the waning days of the French and Indian War marched through the city of New York.

Since then, St. Patrick's Day has become more of an Irish-American holiday than an Irish one. Charities in Boston, Savannah, and Charleston helped initiate the popularity of the holiday was a way to celebrate the Irish heritage.

♣ ♣ ♣

Celebration odds and ends

Canada's oldest and longest running parade is in Montreal. The first parade for St. Patrick's Day occurred there in 1824.

Of the 100 parades in America celebrating the day, the New York Saint Patrick's Day parade and the Boston Saint Patrick's Day parade are the two largest.

One of the largest ever St. Patrick's Day parades in America occurred in Savannah, Georgia in 2006. More than 750,000 spectators showed up for this classic parade.

♣ ♣ ♣

Celebration matches

Match the town with the St. Patrick's Day celebration it is known for.

_____ Buffalo

A. crowns a Sweet Potato Queen

_____ Cleveland

B. onions, carrots, and cabbage are thrown

_____ Detroit

C. largest parade west of the Mississippi

_____ Jackson

D. has two official parades

_____ New Orleans

E. the parade is held in the Corktown section, named for county Cork

_____ San Diego

F. this parade features a Mother of the Year winner

♣ ♣ ♣

Matching Answers

Buffalo (D) has two official parades

Cleveland (F) this parade features a Mother of the Year winner

Detroit (E) the parade is held in the Corktown section, named for county Cork

Jackson (A) crowns a Sweet Potato Queen

New Orleans (B) onions, carrots, and cabbage are thrown

San Diego (C) largest parade west of the Mississippi

♣ ♣ ♣

The Saint Patrick's Day parade in New York City incorporates 150,000 to 200,000 marchers. Automobiles and floats are prohibited.

St. Patrick down under! While not always known for its Irish celebrations, Sydney, Australia actually holds the largest St. Patrick's celebration in the Southern Hemisphere.

♣ ♣ ♣

The city of Brotherly Love has held serve to many things, including the birth of the Declaration of Independence and the Liberty Bell. However, Philadelphia has a connection to St. Patrick's Day. It is home to the second oldest St. Patty's day parade in the United States. The parade has gone on continuously since 1771.

♣ ♣ ♣

Short rounds!

Boulder Colorado and Hot Springs Arkansas both claim to have the shortest St. Patrick's Day parade in America. Although the battle rages on, *Ripley's Believe It Or Not* originally declared the Hot Springs parade the shortest in the 1940s.

However, in recent years, *The Guinness World Book* has crowned its own winner. It declares the Maryville, Missouri parade the shortest in the United States. It is only a half-block.

♣ ♣ ♣

St. Patrick's Day is considered a provincial holiday in Labrador and Newfoundland in Canada.

♣ ♣ ♣

Love that green water!

Dyeing the Chicago River green is a custom that began back in 1962 under the direction of Chicago St. Patrick's Day parade organizer named Stephen Bailey. Bailey, who was also the head of the plumbing union, noticed how a green dye used by plumbers stained a plumber's clothing green. He also noticed it had power to flow with water well because it was used to trace illegal dumping into drains. As a show of unity with Ireland, the river was dyed green...and has been ever since. And no need to worry about the environmental impact. It is minimal.

Incidentally, ever wonder how much dye is used to turn the Chicago River green. It takes about 40 pounds. However, back in the old days, about 100 pounds of the dye were used.

♣ ♣ ♣

Monteserrat, a Carribean Island, considers St. Patrick's Day a national holiday. The island was the home of many people from Ireland. Each year, the island is host to parades, where participants dress up in masks and march through streets.

♣ ♣ ♣

In O'Neill, Nebraska, home of the largest painted shamrock in the world (on an intersection), residents hold a parade, festivities, and conduct a reading of *Green Eggs and Ham* by Dr. Seuss.

O'Neill is nicknamed the "Irish capital of Nebraska." It is named for Irish immigrant John O'Neill. He served in the American Civil war and later moved to Nebraska with three groups of people from Ireland. Incidentally, he was not a general by rank...he gave the title to himself.

♣ ♣ ♣

"When Irish Eyes Are Smiling"

"When Irish Eyes Are Smiling" is another standard song for St. Patrick's Day. Here are a few tidbits you may not have known about the song.

• The song is actually an American song, not Irish. It was written by Chauncey Olcott and George Graff Jr. with music by Ernest Ball. None of them were Irish; but they were vaudeville performers and songwriters.

• Olcott first performed the song in the play *The Isle of Dreams* on January 27, 1913. The show was so unsuccessful that it lasted hardly a month (it closed February 22 the same year).

• The song has long outlasted the show it was in. In 1923, John McCormack made the first recording on the song and helped launch its widespread popularity.

• The song is currently considered part of the public domain.

♣ ♣ ♣

Irish Legacy

Life is like a cup of tea
It is all in how you make it

-Irish proverb

Only more people in the United States claim to be of German heritage than Irish heritage. About 34.7 million Americans trace their heritage back to Ireland. That is about seven times the size of the population of Ireland.

♣ ♣ ♣

Irish is the leading ancestry of people in Delaware, New Hampshire, and Massachusetts.

♣ ♣ ♣

When Irish eyes are....baking beans? While 11 percent of the U.S. population claims to be of Irish heritage, in Massachusetts about 23 percent of the population claims to be connected to the Emerald isle.

♣ ♣ ♣

The two largest counties with Irish heritage are Middlesex County, in Massachusetts, which has nearly 350,000 people of Irish ancestry and Norfolk, also in Massachusetts, which has a little over 200,000.

♣ ♣ ♣

Celebrating Patrick...sports style

See how well you know the answers to these St. Patrick's related sporting questions.

1. Which National League baseball team was the first professional baseball team to wear St. Patrick's Day hats?

2. Which team was the first American League team to wear a St. Patrick's Day hat?

3. What four professional basketball teams have St. Patrick's Day jerseys?

4. What hockey team in the NHL wears a throwback jersey for St. Patrick's Day?

♣ ♣ ♣

Answers

1. The Cincinnati Reds started the tradition of wearing St. Patrick's Day hats in 1978.

2. The Red Sox, who wore St. Patrick's Day hats beginning in 1990. They were the second team to don such hats.

3. The Toronto Raptors, the Chicago Bulls, the New York Knicks, and, of course, the Boston Celtics have special jerseys for St. Patrick's Day.

4. The New Jersey Devils - ironically enough - wear a throwback jersey that had green (which was eliminated from the jersey in 1992). They wear it near or on St. Patrick's Day.

♣ ♣ ♣

Must See TV - HOSS AND THE LEPRECHAUNS

Hoss And The Leprechauns has long been considered a must see TV show. A classic episode of the 1960s western *Bonanza*, the episode is often shown on cable networks on St. Patrick's Day.

The story tells the tale of Hoss Cartwright (played by Dan Blocker), who, while fishing one day, stumbles upon a band of rogue Leprechauns wandering the woods. He returns to Virginia City and explains what he has seen. While no one believes him, a professor named McCarthy, who speaks with an Irish brogue, seems quite interested in Hoss's tale and tells him that capturing a Leprechaun is lucky...because the Leprechaun will give up his secret treasure.

What follows is one of the most raucous episodes of the series, as Hoss, his brothers, his father, and a whirlwind of gold seekers begin hunting for these Leprechauns...who turn out to be acrobats from a circus.

If you have never seen this show, make sure to carve out some room for it on your next St. Patrick's Day. It truly is a show to behold!

Some things to know about the episode...

It actually debuted around Christmas time (December 22, 1963).

It is called Hoss and the Green Manikins in Germany,

It won an Eddie award for editing.

It features a wild stunt by Hoss, falling down the stairs.

♣ ♣ ♣

St. Patrick

"We ought to fish well and diligently, as our Lord exhorts. Hence, we spread out nets so that a great multitude and through me be caught for God."

- St. Patrick

♣ ♣ ♣

Patrick is his name? Patrick's name was actually Maewyn Succut (a.k.a Magonus Scatus). He was later baptized Patricus upon his returned to Britain. Patricus is his Latin name.

Incidentally, Patricus means pertaining to a father or fatherly.

♣ ♣ ♣

Snake-eyes.

The beloved saint may have been credited with ridding Ireland of snakes...but he did not. The land never had snakes. The waters surrounding the island were too cold to ever support a snake crossing from the nearby country of England. So, Ireland has been sans snakes for some time, or at least since the last Ice Age, when it became too cold for the island to support snakes.

While it may seem special that Ireland has no native snake species, neither does Greenland, Hawaii, Iceland, or New Zealand.

♣ ♣ ♣

St. Patrick may be the patron saint of Ireland, but he actually is a native of Great Britain. He was born around 385 AD and lived in either Scotland or Wales (sources debate where he may have lived, but it is generally thought to be Banwen, Wales). His parents were actually Roman citizens named Calpurnius and Conchess who lived in the Empire's northern lands.

♣ ♣ ♣

St. Patrick's defining moment may have come when he was kidnapped at the age of 16 and taken to Ireland by a band of men led by Niall of the Nine Hostages. Not much is known about Niall, though he is listed as one of the high kings of Ireland.

Patrick spent at least six years as a slave for an Irish shepherd who practiced the Druidic religion. Some people believed he was kidnapped on March 17 in the year 432 AD.

♣ ♣ ♣

St. Patrick is believed to have received a calling from above. God, spoke to Patrick during a dream urging him to leave Ireland. Patrick escaped his captivity at age 22 and returned to England...though he stopped in France just long enough to learn about the priesthood.

♣ ♣ ♣

St. Patrick went to France and studied in a monastery under a man named St. Germain, a bishop of the region called Auxerre. Patrick remained in the monastery for twelve years and became convinced that he had to return to Ireland to convert the local pagan population.

Patrick declared that an angel had convinced him to return. The angel came to him in a dream and told him to return to Ireland and preach God's word there.

♣ ♣ ♣

St. Patrick also has several islands named for him. The most famous is located off the coast of Ireland.

The island is known for its bramble bushes in grass. Birds such as cormorants, herring gulls, and shag also nest there.

♣ ♣ ♣

St. Patrick founded his first church in Ireland at Mag-inis. It is considered a sacred region today.

♣ ♣ ♣

A horse of a different color?

Although St. Patrick's Day is usually celebrated with dashes of green, St. Patrick himself was known for wearing blue vestments.

To this day, several shades of blue are called St. Patrick's blue, including a sky blue color that is popular in England. The people of Ireland often associate a darker blue with the saint.

♣ ♣ ♣

Beat the drums!

According to legend, St. Patrick pounded drums as a way to rid Ireland of its snake infestation. The legend states that snakes attacked him when he was on a 40 day fast in the hills.

However, scientists believe that no snakes have lived in Ireland since the last Ice Age. The slow worm, a form of legless lizard, is the closest animal to a native snake in Ireland.

♣ ♣ ♣

St. Patrick is believed to have a scared role as Patron Saint of Ireland. He is believed to look down on the Irish as well as help decide which Irish people enter heaven.

♣♣♣

St. Patrick is believed to have consecrated more than 300 bishops in Ireland.

Although St. Patrick is believed to have used the three-leaf shamrock to teach about the Holy Trinity, some people believe if he saw a four-leaf clover, he would use the fourth leaf to represent God's grace.

♣ ♣ ♣

An old legend says that the seas around Ireland are so rough because of all the serpents St. Patrick sent there.

♣ ♣ ♣

Slemish is the Irish name for St. Patrick Mountain. Legend has it that St. Patrick was enslaved as a shepherd on this mountain and first heard the voice of God here. Many people make the pilgrimage to the top of the mountain every year of March 17th.

The mountain is located in Antrim, Northern Ireland and stretches 1,434 feet. Incidentally, it is the remains of the lava plug of an extinct volcano.

It later became the site of a camp of United Irish soldiers in the 1798 rebellion in County Antrim.

♣ ♣ ♣

An end to slavery! St. Patrick is sometimes believed to be the first person in Ireland to speak out against slavery. Part of this is due to the fact that he could speak from his own personal experience.

In fact, the slave trade on the island was alleged to have ended shortly after his death.

♣ ♣ ♣

Most Irish believe that St. Patrick was buried in Dun-lethglaisse, on a spot that two oxen, carrying his body, chose to stop (it appears, prior to this, that followers of the saint did not know where to bury him).

Some Englanders claim that Patrick was buried at the Abbey of Glastonbury where he had moved to live out his final days.

♣ ♣ ♣

The Cathedral in Armagh, part of the St. Patrick's Church of Ireland, rests on land called the "Ridge of the Willow Tree."

Local lore has it that St. Patrick was given this land by a man named Daire. Daire was an Irish chief that St. Patrick brought back to life.

Stories claim that, prior to reviving the man, Patrick asked Daire for land to build a church. Daire asked him which land he would prefer and Patrick replied, "The height of land which is Dorcum Salicis" which was Gaelic for Ridge of the Willow Tree. Daire refused. However, once Patrick saved his life, he was truly indebted.

The legend also suggests that Patrick also brought Daire's horse back to life as well.

♣ ♣ ♣

St. Patrick has some lesser known duties. He is the patron saint of engineers and the patron saint of Nigeria.

♣ ♣ ♣

Claddagh Rings

Claddagh rings have been a traditional Irish wedding ring since the 1600s. Dating back to the times of the Roman Empire, the rings were originally called "fede rings," and are symbolic of faithful love to one another.

The rings are sometimes related to the ancient Celtic myths. The right side is considered to be Dadga, the father of the Celts while the left hand is said to be Anu, the mother of the Celts. Some people claim the original Claddagh ring is said to be a gift from an eagle to a woman named Margaret Joyce who did not waste her inheritance, but used it to help the people of Ireland.

The Claddagh ring has been a symbol of love for centuries. In the 1800s, when people departed Ireland for America, often they took a Claddagh ring as the one thing of value that they loved as a reminder of their homeland. The rings are still popular to this day – with men and women – and are often passed down in families.

♣ ♣ ♣

St. Patrick's Day facts

"May the roof above us never fall in and may we friends beneath it never fall out."

- Traditional Irish blessing

♣ ♣ ♣

Have a pint! A common custom calls for people to raise a pint of Guinness beer on St. Patrick's Day. And it truly is a custom. According to the Guinness Company, on average, 5.5 million pints of beer are lifted on a typical day. That number skyrockets to 13 million pints on March 17. Incidentally, this company also started the Guinness Book of Word Records.

♣ ♣ ♣

St. Patrick's day is a traditional holiday on Boston. Schools are even closed. However, it is not just to honor the close heritage that Boston shares with Irish immigrants. It commemorates the day that the American army, under George Washington, watched the British evacuate Boston during the Revolutionary War and head to Nova Scotia. The day is called "Evacuation Day" in Beantown.

♣ ♣ ♣

Money making holiday! St. Patrick's Day has turned into a money-making business in modern times. Cards, decorations, and souvenirs help celebrate buyers celebrate the holiday. More than 4.14 billion dollars are spent on the holiday in America alone.

♣ ♣ ♣

It is often said that if you do not wear green on St. Patrick's Day, you have the right to be pinched.

♣ ♣ ♣

Americans send about 8 million St. Patrick's Day cards each year.

Popular topics include:

• Leprechauns
• Shamrocks
• Gold
• Symbols of Luck
• Rainbows

♣ ♣ ♣

Thanks Uncle Walt!

Leprechauns became more closely associated with St. Patrick's Day with the help of Walt Disney. In the classic movie *Darby O'Gill and the Little People*, complete with pre-James Bond Sean Connery, writers established a connection between the "little people" and St. Patrick's Day.

♣♣♣

Darby O' Gill and the Little People

Darby O'Gill had long been a pet project of Walt Disney. He had been working on a story about Ireland since World War II. The war made it difficult to produce the movie. However, following the formal end of the war, Walt went to Ireland in December, 1948. He let the people of the Emerald Isle in on the fact he was making a movie about Leprechauns. He tentatively titled the movie "The Little People." It was about ten years before he made the movie. But, he sent Disney employees to the island to start making scenes for the flick.

Disney kept the movie somewhat secretive. He never even credited the people who played the Leprechauns in the movie; preferring people think that he had infiltrated their kingdom. In an episode of *Walt Disney's Wonderful World of Color*, he gives secret insights into the making of the movie. He explains that he even captured the king of the Leprechauns.

Disney's movie came out about one year after the copyright expired on the stories that it was based. These stories were written by Herminie Templeton Kavanagh.

Sean Connery was spotted in this movie by Albert Broccoli (of James Bond movie fame) and quickly became Broccoli's choice for the role of the super spy. Sean actually sings a duet with Disney actress Janet Munro. The song was even released on a single. However, if you do meet Sean Connery, don't bring up the song...it was his least favorite part of the movie.

♣ ♣ ♣

The numbers have it. About 39 percent of the American population celebrates St. Patrick's Day. Of that number about 83 percent wear green and 25 percent decorate their home or work space.

♣ ♣ ♣

Say hey Patrick. According to the U.S. Census, the name Patrick has been given to about 650,000 children during the past century in America.

Some famous Patricks in America are:

• Patrick Kennedy
• Patrick Dempsey
• Patrick Ewing
• Patrick Warburton
• Patrick Henry
• Patrick Adcock

♣ ♣ ♣

Until the 1970s, pubs in Ireland were closed on St. Patrick's Day because it was a national religious holiday.

Some of the popular drinks include:

Black and Tan
Bushmill's Irish Buck
Lucky Leprechaun
Emerald Isle
Shandy

♣ ♣ ♣

Irish Lore

May neighbors respect you,
Trouble neglect you,
The angels protect you,
And heaven accept you.

- Traditional Irish Blessing

The lucky penny of the Irish dates back to a time when a seller gave back a penny – or a portion of a sale price – in a sale.

The modern Irish penny debuted on February 15, 1971. This is officially called Decimal Day, the day when Ireland switched to decimal currency. The penny was part of Irish currency until it was replaced by the Euro in 2000.

♣ ♣ ♣

The Irish flag is red, white, and orange to show the unity that the Irish hope comes to their country:

Green represents Irish Catholics.

Orange represents Irish Protestants.

White represents the hope that they may someday get together.

♣ ♣ ♣

Ireland has many nicknames, including:

The Emerald Isle
The Bower
The Old Sod
The Four Green Fields
Land of Erin
The Three Kingdoms
The Green Island
The Land of Green

Officially Irish. Then, the only green you would wear on St. Patrick's Day is a shamrock on your lapel.

♣♣♣

There are no postal zipcodes in Ireland once you get out of Cork and Dublin. Ireland is the only member of the European Union that does not have a postal code system and one of the few countries internationally that does not.

How do they address those letters? Typically the address is listed by the county, nearest post town, and then by the townland.

However, in the spring 2015, this will probably be changed.

♣ ♣ ♣

Cats were often considered unlucky in ancient Ireland. It stems from a time when wild cats lived in the Dunmore caves of the Emerald Isle.

According to an old legend from St. Malachy, stated in the 12th century, Ireland would become fully at peace when "the shamrock meets the palm." This referred to peace coming when St. Patrick's Day falls on Palm Sunday.

This is unlikely to happen for a major reason. The Catholic Church has control over the actual feast day and although it is traditionally fixed on March 17th, it can be moved to avoid coinciding with Palm Sunday.

In fact, in 1940, it was moved to Wednesday, April 3 to avoid being celebrated with Palm Sunday. In 2008, it was officially celebrated on Saturday, March 15 to avoid Holy Monday.

♣ ♣ ♣

It is believed that Irish immigrants brought oatmeal to America. As a result, Americans have greatly profited from the health benefits associated with oatmeal. These include its supposed ability to help lower cholesterol.

♣ ♣ ♣

Cork is the largest county in Ireland. Louth is the smallest.

Other extremes include:

Sunniest spot: Rosslare in the county of Wexford
Driest spot: Dublin City (with less than 800 mm rain per year)
Cloudiest spot: Omagh in the county of Tyrone

Local lore suggests that St. Patrick's jawbone was kept preserved in a silver shrine located in County Down. It was often brought out to cure a person of epileptic seizures or provide help during childbirth. On a rare occasion, it was brought out to help victims of the legendary evil eye.

♣ ♣ ♣

Dripsey, in County Cork, was the home of the shortest St. Patrick's parade in 1999. The parade was about 75 feet long, as parade participants went from one pub to another.

♣ ♣ ♣

Stop by for a pint. The island of Ireland has more than 10,000 pubs.

♣♣♣

A bit about the language:

The Irish Alphabet has only 18 letters. The letters J, K, Q, V, W, X, Y and Z are not used.

The language itself is called Irish, Gaelic, or Irish Gaelic.

About 76 percent of the people in the country speak Irish.

The official name of the Irish language – in Ireland – is Gaeilge

Ireland is the twentieth largest island in the world.

The tin whistle is considered a traditional Irish instrument. It was developed in Europe as long as 35,000 years ago or more and refined over time. By the mid 1800s, it had become a popular instrument with Irish and Celtic musicians. The name "tin whistle" actually dates back to 1825. Before that, it was known as the penny whistle.

♣ ♣ ♣

Ireland began to call itself Ireland in the 7th century. Northerners of the land helped promote the name change. It is believed that it was named for Queen Eire who ruled the land centuries before.

Irish lions! The original MGM lion was an Irish lion. He was named Cairbre and born in the Dublin Zoo in 1919 (some say 1927). Cedric Gibbons, who worked for Sam Goldwyn (the G in MGM) brought the lion to the movie mogul's attention. Incidentally, Cedric supposedly helped design the Academy Award.

In Irish, the name Cairbre means charioteer. His name was changed to Slats when he came to America. He lived until 1936. You will know you have spotted the original because he was the lion that looked around at the beginning of MGM movies – but remained silent. Subsequent ones roared.

♣ ♣ ♣

Count O'Dracula? The oldest tales of vampires actually trace themselves back to Ireland.

♣ ♣ ♣

Shamrock Shake

Depending on when you were born – or where you live – some of you may know what the shamrock shake is and others may have no clue.

The shamrock shake was the brainchild of *McDonald's*. Appearing in 1970, the shake was the idea of Roger's Marketing firm. They used a family recipe by James Byrne, an executive artist at the company, to help manufacture the shake as a seasonal alternative to *McDonald's* traditional shakes.

The shakes were a seasonal delight for decades. In 1974, proceeds from the sale of some Shamrock Shakes helped fund the first Ronald McDonald House. In the 1980s, they were served in special cups feature Uncle O'Grimacey. McDonalds even had a short-lived encounter with Shamrock Sundaes from 1980 to 1981.

However, in the 1990s, they began to disappear from *McDonald's* throughout the country. They have made an appearance in recent years, but not in all markets. For example, they are available throughout the New England states from mid-February to mid-March, but they can be difficult to find in New York.

♣ ♣ ♣

Legend has it the Patrick Maguire was the first person of Christopher Columbus's crew to physically set foot on America. He was Irish born.

♣ ♣ ♣

The Murphy's have it. Murphy is the most common last name – or surname – in Ireland.

The rest are

2. Kelly
3. O'Sullivan
4. Walsh
5. O'Brien
6. Byrne
7. Ryan
8. O'Connor
9. O'Neill
10. O' Reilly

♣ ♣ ♣

St. Patrick's Day Jokes

1. What do people from Hawaii give to visitors on St. Patrick's Day?
A: Shil-lei-leis

2. What is a leprechaun's favorite music?
A. Shamrock and roll

3. What is the official whale of Ireland?
A. Sham-mu

4. What is a leprechaun's favorite vegetable?
A. Lepre-corn

5. What should young children watch on TV on St. Patrick's Day?
A. Blarney the dinosaur

6. Why did the leprechaun stop playing music?
A. Someone was always harping on him to quick making a racket.

7. Where should you rest on St. Patrick's Day?
A. On your padd-io.

♣ ♣ ♣

How Many Words Can You Make From….

St. Patrick's Day

♣ ♣ ♣

Four movies to see on St. Patrick's Day

The Quiet Man (1952) with John Wayne and Maureen O'Hara

Darby O'Gill and the Little People (1959) with Sean Connery

Far and Away (1992) with Tom Cruise and Nicole Kidman

Leap Year (2010) with Amy Adams

♣ ♣ ♣

SOURCES

Austin, C. "The Meaning of Green and Other Facts About St. Patrick's Day." URL:
{ HYPERLINK "http://merganser.math.gvsu.edu/myth/meaninggreen.html" }

"Blarney Stone." Sacred Sites website. URL: { HYPERLINK
"http://sacredsites.com/europe/ireland/blarney_stone_facts.html" }

"Caiebre." Irish Baby Names.com { HYPERLINK "http://irish-baby-names.com/2012/11/cairbre-the-lion-in-the-movies/" }

"Colcannon." Irish central website. URL: { HYPERLINK "http://www.irishcentral.com/culture/food-drink/colcannon-traditional-irish-recipe-118184429-237376811.html" }

"Darby O'Gill and the Little People". IMBd.com. URL: { HYPERLINK
"http://www.imdb.com/title/tt0052722/trivia" }

"Darby O'Gill and the Little People." Turner Classic Movies website. URL: { HYPERLINK
"http://www.tcm.com/tcmdb/title/72263/Darby-O-Gill-and-the-Little-People/trivia.html" }

History Channel. "St. Patrick's Day Facts." URL:
{ HYPERLINK "http://www.history.com/topics/st-patricks-day-facts" }

"Hoss and the Leprechauns." TV.show.com. URL: { HYPERLINK
"http://www.tv.com/shows/bonanza/hoss-and-the-leprechauns-98534/" }

"Irish Names." Irishcentral.com
URL.http://www.irishcentral.com/roots/genealogy/the-10-most-popular-irish-last-names-98012749-237788291.html#

Irish Culture and Customs. URL: { HYPERLINK
"http://www.irishcultureandcustoms.com/TriviaDidyouknow1.html" }

Irish Facts. Fantasy Ireland website. URL: { HYPERLINK "http://www.fantasy-ireland.com/claddagh-history.html" \l "axzz2LLkMgT9w" }

Irish Facts and Trivia. Sons of Erin website. URL: { HYPERLINK
"http://www.sonsoferin.com/content/irish-facts-and-trivia" }

♣ ♣ ♣

"Irish Instruments." URL: { HYPERLINK "http://www.stmoroky.com/reviews/music/irinst.htm" }

"Irish Language." Ominglot.com. URL: { HYPERLINK "http://www.omniglot.com/writing/irish.htm" }

Irish Symbols. URL: { HYPERLINK "http://www.livingartsoriginals.com/irish-song.html" }

Jenkins, Elizabeth. "St. Patrick's Day Tradition." Better Homes and Gardens website. URL: { HYPERLINK "http://www.bhg.com/holidays/st-patricks-day/traditions/st-patricks-day-traditions/" \l "page=14" }

"March 17th events in history." Brainhistory.com. URL: { HYPERLINK "http://www.brainyhistory.com/days/march_17.html" }

"O'Neill History." City of ONeill Website. http://www.cityofoneill.com/history.html

Quiz for St. Patrick's Day. Holidayspot.com. URL: { HYPERLINK "http://www.theholidayspot.com/patrick/quiz.htm" }

Roach, John. "St. Patrick's Day 2012: Facts, Myths, and Opinions." National Geographic News. URL: { HYPERLINK "http://news.nationalgeographic.com/news/2012/03/120316-saint-patricks-day-2012-march-17-facts-ireland-irish-nation/" }

"Seven Crazy St. Patrick's Day traditions." Discovery.com. URL: *dsc.discovery.com* > { HYPERLINK "http://dsc.discovery.com/adventure/" }

"Shamrocks for St. Patricks." Riverdeep.net. URL: { HYPERLINK "http://www.riverdeep.net/current/2002/03/031102_stpatrick.jhtml" }

"Shamrock Shake." AboutMacDonalds.com. URL: { HYPERLINK "http://www.aboutmcdonalds.com/mcd/our_company/amazing_stories/food/the_shamrock_shake.html" }

"Shamrock Shake." Wikipedia. URL: { HYPERLINK "http://en.wikipedia.org/wiki/Shamrock_Shake" }

St. Patrick's Day Around the World. Holidayspot.com. URL: { HYPERLINK "http://www.theholidayspot.com/patrick/around_the_world.htm" }

St. Patrick's Day by the numbers. History.com. URL; { HYPERLINK "http://www.history.com/topics/st-patricks-day-facts/interactives/st-patricks-day-by-the-numbers" }

♣ ♣ ♣

St. Patrick's Day Fun Facts. WSAW Channel 7.com
URL: { HYPERLINK "http://www.wsaw.com/seasonal/misc/40129602.html" }

St. Patrick's Day Fun Facts: Beyond the Blarney. National Geogrphic.com. URL: { HYPERLINK "http://news.nationalgeographic.com/news/2005/03/0315_050315_stpatricksday_2.html" }

St. Patrick's Day History.... The Whiskey Connection Explained. About.com. URL: { HYPERLINK "http://homecooking.about.com/od/foodhistory/a/stpatdayhistory.htm" }

"St. Patrick's Day Symbols and Traditions." History.com. URL: { HYPERLINK "http://www.history.com/topics/st-patricks-day-symbols-and-traditions" }

"St. Patrick's Day: Top Ten Facts." UK Telegraph. URL: { HYPERLINK "http://www.telegraph.co.uk/news/worldnews/europe/ireland/5005127/St-Patricks-Day-Top-10-facts.html" }

St. Patrick's Day Trivia. Aiming Low.com. URL: { HYPERLINK "http://aiminglow.com/2012/03/st-patricks-day-fun-facts/" }

"St. Patrick's Day Trivia." Realsimple.com. URL: { HYPERLINK "http://www.realsimple.com/holidays-entertaining/holidays/more-holidays/test-st-pattys-day-iq-10000001720652/index.html" }

"St. Patrick's Day Trivia Quiz." Chicago Tribune. URL: { HYPERLINK "http://www.chicagotribune.com/sns-holiday-st-patricks-quiz,0,6954078,post.triviaquiz" }

"St. Patrick's Day Times and Dates." Time and Date.com. URL: { HYPERLINK "http://www.timeanddate.com/holidays/us/st-patrick-day" }

♣ ♣ ♣

Stokes, George Thomas. Ireland and the Celtic Church. Hodder and Stoughton, 1924.

"Top Fifty St. Patrick's Day Facts." St, Patricksday.com. URL: { HYPERLINK "http://www.stpatricksday.com/history/stpatrick/50-facts.shtml" }

"Top Ten Little Known Facts About Ireland." URL: { HYPERLINK "http://www.irishcentral.com/roots/Top-ten-little-known-facts-about-Ireland-ahead-of-the-Gathering-2013-173265331.html" }

"When Irish eyes are Smiling." Songfacts.com. URL: { HYPERLINK "http://www.songfacts.com/detail.php?id=15042" }

"Which Came First?" Ye Olde Woburn. URL: http://www.yeoldewoburn.net/chronpatrick.pdf

"Why Ireland Had No Snakes." Popsci.com URL: { HYPERLINK "http://www.popsci.com/why-doesnt-ireland-have-snakes" }

♣ ♣ ♣

THANK YOU FOR READING – HAPPY SAINT PATRICK'S DAY!!!

REMEMBERING THOSE WHO ARE IRISH, IF ONLY ON ST. PATRICK'S DAY.

THANK YOU GREAT GRANDMOTHER ANNIE KEEGAN FOR COMING TO AMERICA FROM IRELAND.

♣ ♣ ♣